TRA JP

£4-00 33/24

031140 052635

KU-114-136

Last years of British steam

First series

Compiled by G. FREEMAN ALLEN

LONDON

IAN ALLAN

INTRODUCTION

From 17,000 odd at the start of the Modernisation Plan, British Railways' steam locomotive fleet has already been decimated to well below 3,000. If one counts the former Eastern south of Shaftholme Junction as a separate Region and ignores its 1967 merger with the North Eastern, three Regions of the system are already bare of steam power. The Scottish Region is on the brink of eliminating steam as this book is prepared. And only in the industrial North of England are the last pockets of steam hanging on—or perhaps one should say hanging together, in view of the meagre upkeep the engines are getting. In some cases even the sheds that house them are literally falling to pieces.

It was only to be expected that this rapid decline of steam would redouble the energy of enthusiast photographers to record scenes and impressions that would soon become nostalgic memories. The variety of types may have dwindled these past few years. But at the same time the art of railway photography has broadened. Although the great flow of prints covers fewer designs of locomotives, the varied approaches of today's photographers have added a more than compensating appeal, which I hope is reflected in this portfolio.

Certainly I have enormously enjoyed browsing through the publisher's files to assemble the collection. Like any anthology, it cannot avoid expressing the compiler's own tastes, but I have tried to make it representative of all the railway photographic styles developed since the camera became almost a staple of the British railway scene from the late 1940s onwards. Straightforward three-quarter views of engines and trains bearing down on the camera still have a dramatic appeal no less than the impressionism that captures the grimy, gloomy industrial atmosphere in which British railways were born and developed so much of their business.

This collection has touched only the fringe of available photographs. It is hoped to make it the first of a series that will be pleasurable memories of the last years of steam in the all-diesel and electric age to come. Without doubt there is a great deal of excellent material still in private files that has not yet been submitted to publishers. Any photographer with unpublished post-war prints which he would like appraised for future books in this series is warmly invited to send them to the Editor for consideration.

G.F.A.

Title page: WR 4–6–0 No. 7029 *Clun Castle* restarts the Ian Allan "Zulu" Paddington–Birkenhead excursion from Banbury on March 4, 1967.

[*John H. Bird*

Facing page: Class 5 4–6–0 No. 44690 picks up water from Salwick troughs with the 2.40 p.m. Blackpool–Birmingham on October 23, 1966.

[*P. Riley*

Left, upper: WR 4–6–0 No. 4079 *Pendennis Castle* heads
the return Ian Allan "Birkenhead Flyer" excursion
between Chirk and Gobowen on March 4, 1967.
[*J. H. Cooper-Smith*

Left, lower: WR 4–6–0 No. 7029 *Clun Castle* gathers speed.
[*A. Clarke*

Above: WR 4–6–0 No. 6956 *Mottram Hall* heads a freight
towards Didcot near Radley on a November morning
in 1965.
[*J. A. M. Vaughan*

Above: "Royal Scot" 4-6-0 No. 46115 *Scots Guardsman* emerges from Calton Tunnel soon after departure with the 9.50 Edinburgh Waverley–Carlisle on July 17, 1965.

[*P. Riley.*

Below: A WR "King" 4-6-0 heads for Paddington with an up South Wales express on a July morning in 1961.

[*G. F. Heiron.*

Above: Class A3 4–6–2 No. 60084 *Trigo* storms out of York on a troop special on August 15, 1964.
[*C. P. Walker*

Right upper: Class A2/3 Pacific No. 60521 *Watling Street* at York.
[*J. D. Critchlow*

Right lower: Class B16/3 4–6–0 No. 61454 heads a Scarborough excursion at York on July 27, 1963.
[*C. P. Walker*

Left: Evening studies of Class Q6 0–8–0s on Newcastle High Level Bridge in March, 1966.

[*M. Dunnett*

Above: Class 5 4–6–0 No. 45101 at Stockport Edgley in November, 1965.

[*D. Mackinnon*

Right: On shed—Class A4 4–6–2 No. 60007 *Sir Nigel Gresley.*

[*P. Hocquard*

Left: Class D16/3 4–4–0 No. 62530 heads the 4.31 p.m. Lincoln train out of Doncaster on July 4, 1958.

[*R. K. Evans*

Below: The 5.51 p.m. Okehampton–Padstow takes the North Cornwall line at Meldon Junction behind Class T9 4–4–0 No. 30313.

[*S. C. Nash*

Right: Class 2 4–4–0 No. 40663 on Kittybrewster shed, May 6, 1957.

[*R. K. Evans*

Below: Pickersgill 4–4–0 No. 54486 pilots a Class 4 2–6–4T with the morning Perth–Blair Atholl local through Kingswood loop in August, 1960.

[*W. J. V. Anderson*

Above: Class 3 2–6–2T No. 82005 crosses Barmouth Bridge on August 13, 1963, with a Barmouth-bound train.
[*T. Boustead*

Right: Afonwen on April 7, 1961: Class 3 2–6–2T No. 82000, on the right, arrives with the 9.27 from Barmouth to meet WR Class 2251 0–6–0 No. 2287 on the 10.25 a.m. from Pwllheli.
[*R. E. James-Robertson*

Below: A Class 2 2–6–0 pilots a WR "Manor" 4–6–0 near Commins Coch with the Saturday 9.25 Pwllheli–Paddington on August 23, 1958.
[*L. N. Owen*

Left: Class 4 4–6–0 No. 75033 attacks the 1 in 52 to Talerddig summit with the last steam-hauled "Cambrian Coast Express" on March 4, 1967. *[P. Riley*

Right: WR 0–6–0PT No. 7405 leaves Dolgellau with the 6.30 p.m. to Barmouth on July 22, 1961. *[A. H. Bryant*

Below: Class 3 2–6–2T No. 82033 pulls out of Barmouth on August 7, 1963. *[T. Boustead*

Left upper: A Class 3 2–6–2 approaches Portmadoc with the 3.45 p.m.
Barmouth–Pwllheli on July 31, 1964.

[*M. Dunnett*

Left lower: A WR "Dukedog" 4–4–0 pauses at Harlech with a Pwllheli–Machynlleth
train on July 27, 1956.

[*R. E. Vincent*

Above: WR 4–6–0 No. 7822 *Foxcote Manor* leaves Machynlleth with an Aberystwyth
train in September, 1964.

[*M. Pope*

Above: An SR Class O2 0–4–4T heads a Pier Head train out of Ryde Esplanade, Isle of Wight, on June 21, 1965.

[*M. Dunnett*

Left: Class O2 0–4–4T No. W20 *Shanklin* enters Ryde St Johns Road with the 5.5 p.m. Ryde–Ventnor on June 18, 1965.

[*M. Dunnett*

Above: Class 02 0-4-4T No. W22 *Brading* starts
a down train out of Ryde St Johns Road on
August 22, 1964.

[*M. S. Welch*

Right: Isle of Wight Class 02 0-4-4Ts on shed
at Ryde, December 12, 1966.

[*J. A. M. Vaughan*

Above: SR Class USA 0–6–0 No. 30072 takes water at Wimbledon during an enthusiasts' special working on October 9, 1966.

[*J. H. Jones*

Below: WR 0–6–0 PT No. 3728 shunts at Lydbrook Junction, on the branch from Ross-on-Wye, April 14, 1964.

[*B. J. Ashworth*

Above: SR Adams 4–4–2Ts Nos. 30584 and 30853 climb to Combpyne with the 4.36 p.m. Axminster–Lyme Regis on June 6, 1960.

[*S. C. Nash*

Below: The WR 0–4–2Ts Nos. 1442 and 1450 take water at Axminster in February, 1965, on their way from Yeovil to work the Seaton branch.

[*Ivo Peters*

Left: Class A2/3 Pacific No. 60514 *Chamossaire* makes an unsteady start from Peterborough with a Kings Cross train.

[*W. A. Corkill*

Above: Stanier Pacific No. 46240 *City of Coventry* pauses at Rugby with the 9.32 Wolverhampton–Euston on August 17, 1963.

[*C. P. Walker*

Left, upper : WR 4–6–0 No. 6988 *Swithland Hall* skirts the sea wall between
Teignmouth and Dawlish with a troop special on August 8, 1956.

[*R. J. Blenkinsop*

Left, lower : The 12.25 a.m. Manchester–Penzance, headed by WR 4–6–0
No. 4080 *Powderham Castle,* heads out of Newton Abbot on October 6, 1959.

[*D. S. Fish*

Above : WR 2–6–0 No. 5339 climbs Dainton bank, west of Newton Abbot,
with a down freight on May 29, 1957.

[*E. Rixon*

Above: The original Brunel terminus at Bristol Temple Meads on May 22, 1965, with a Class 3 2–6–2T, No. 82004.

[*P. J. Kelley*

Left: Class 4 2–6–0 No. 76052 arrives at Birkenhead Woodside with the 1.12 p.m. from Wrexham on October 21, 1966

[*M. Dunnett*

Above: Class 4 2–6–0 No. 43012 and the 8.18 a.m. from Cheadle Heath in Manchester Central on October 6, 1965.

[*J. Clarke*

Right: "Crab" 2–6–0 No. 42707 ready to leave Bristol Temple Meads with the 6.30 p.m. Birmingham stopping train on August 3, 1963.

[*B. J. Ashworth*

Left: Class V2 2-6-2
No. 60818
leaves Montrose with the
6 p.m. Glasgow–
Aberdeen via Dundee on
August 29, 1965.

[*M. S. Burns*]

Below: A Dundee-bound
goods crosses the Tay
at Perth behind a Class
B1 4-6-0 in April, 1964.

[*W. J. V. Anderson*]

eft upper : Class 4F 0–6–0 No. 44139 climbs the Camp Hill avoiding line in Birmingham
/ith a southbound goods on August 18, 1963.

[*C. P. Walker*

eft lower : Class 9F 2–10–0 No. 92093 strikes out of Preston with
n up goods on March 29, 1967.

[*J. H. Cooper-Smith*

bove : Ex-LNWR 0–8–0 No. 49407 climbs past Sutton Oak, in the West Midlands,
ith a goods on November 30, 1963.

[*P. Riley*

Left, upper : Class 2 2–6–0s Nos.
46426 and 46458 double-head a
Leeds–Workington special out
of Penrith on June 13, 1964.

[*D. Cross*

Left, lower : Ex-LNWR 0–8–0
No. 49406 trundles an up goods
over Dillicar troughs, Tebay,
in July, 1958.

[*W. J. V. Anderson*

Right, upper : WR 2–6–2
No. 4111 leaves Acocks Green
with the 8.33 a.m. Lapworth–
Birmingham on June 13, 1961.

[*M. Mensing*

Right, lower : WR 2–8–0
No. 3834 passes Teignmouth
with an up goods on August 8,
1965.

[*T. E. Williams*

Above: SR Class Q 0–6–0 No. 30545 storms up to Virginia Water, en route from Staines to Reading with an enthusiasts' special on January 3, 1965.

[*B. Stephenson*

Right, upper: A pair of SR Class Q1 0–6–0s, Nos. 33035 and 33040, at Sharnal Street, on the Allhallows-on-Sea branch, on February 4, 1961.

[*E. A. Woollard*

Right, lower: A surprising combination of 0.1 Class 0–6–0 No. 31065 piloting Schools 4–4–0 No. 30934 leaves Ashford (Kent) in charge of the 4.58 p.m. Dover to Tonbridge on a summer Saturday.

[*D. Cross*

Above: Midland compound 4–4–0 No. 41054 heads a Leicester–St Pancras semi-fast past Great Bowden signalbox on August 14, 1954.

[*G. D. King*

Left: WR 4–6–0 No. 1005 *County of Devon* emerges from St Annes Park Tunnel, near Bristol, with a Portsmouth–Cardiff express.

[*G. F. Heiron*

Left : With rear-end assistance from WR 2–6–2 No. 6155, Stanier 2–8–0 No. 48351 restarts a goods from Ledbury on February 4, 1964.

[*A. A. Vickers*

Above : Class 2 2–6–0 No. 78009 heads a Moreton-in-Marsh goods near Longdon Road, on the Shipston-on-Stour branch, on December 29, 1959.   [*H. W. Burchell*

Below : WR 2251 class 0–6–0 No. 2211 starts the 8.43 a.m. to Leamington out of Stratford-upon-Avon in June, 1964.

[*T. E. Williams*

Above: A Chester–Shrewsbury train, headed by Class 5 4–6–0 No. 45116, overtakes Class 9 2–10–0 No. 92016 at Rhosymedre, near Ruabon, on March 4, 1967. *[B. Alexander*

Left: Class V2 2–6–2 No. 60973 leaves Edinburgh Waverley on an Aberdeen express in August, 1965. *[J. M. Dickson*

Left, upper: SR Class
N15 4–6–0 No. 30772
Sir Percivale passes
Micheldever with a
Southampton boat train.

[*F. R. Hebron*

Left, lower: The 9.30 a.m.
Basingstoke–Bourne-
mouth, headed by Class
H15 4–6–0 No. 30475,
near Lymington Junction
on July 31, 1960.

[*D. J. Lane*

Right: SR Class D1
4–4–0 No. 31759 and
Class WC 4–6–2 No.
34083 *605 Squadron*
double-head the 1.10 p.m.
Charing Cross–Ramsgate
through London Bridge
on June 10, 1961.

[*M. Pope*

Class J15 0–6–0 No. 65438 passes Newmarket with the 11.12 a.m.
Mildenhall–Cambridge on May 22, 1958.   [*G. R. Mortimer*

Class B12 4–6–0 No. 61572 approaches Hadley Wood South Tunnel, on the
GN main line out of Kings Cross, with a special on October 5, 1963.
[G. S. Cooks

Norwich in 1955: Class D16/3 4–4–0 No. 62540 passes Class B12/3 4–6–0
No. 61547 departing with a Cromer train.   [P. H. Groom

Class 60? 0-6-0 No. 64608 on Montrose viaduct with the afternoon goods to
Dundee on April 13, 1966.

[*W. B. Alexander*

Below: WR "County" class 4-6-0 and westbound "Cornish Riviera Express"
on Moorswater Viaduct, Liskeard, Cornwall, on June 24, 1955.

[*R. E. Vincent*

WR "Hall" 4–6–0 and westbound freight on St Germans Viaduct,
Cornwall, on July 5, 1951.

[*D. E. H. Box*

Above: WR 0–6–0PT No. 7439 near Felin Fach with the Lampeter–Aberayron branch milk train on September 8, 1963
[*A. Muckley*

Right: A Cinderford branch goods, headed by WR 0–6–0PT No. 8749, climbs past Upper Soudley on August 28, 1964.
[*B. J. Ashworth*

Facing page: Scottish industrial steam—Hunslet 0–6–0ST No. 15 of the Wemyss Railway at Buckhaven in April, 1963.

[*W. J. V. Anderson*

Above: English industrial—preparing for the afternoon's work at Storefield Quarries, Northants, on December 30, 1966: from left to right 0–4–0STs *Cockspur* (by Peckett, 1912), *Enterprise* (by Bagnall, 1907) and No. 20 (by A. Barclay, 1942).

[*G. D. King*

Below: Another Wemyss Railway scene—No. 14 shortly after leaving Wemyss in August, 1964.

[*W. J. V. Anderson*

Left: National Coal Board Barclay 0–6–0T No. 24 of West Ayrshire, fitted with Giesl ejector, shunting at Waterside Colliery on March 2, 1965.
[D. Cross

Below: A Corby iron ore train, headed by a Hunslet 0–6–0ST, on August 6, 1964.
[V. L. Murphy

Right : The NCB's ex-North Staffordshire Railway 0–6–2T No. 2 pilots Giesl ejector-fitted Hunslet 0–6–0ST *Charles* at Sandhole Washery in April, 1965.
[*W. J. V. Anderson*

Below : Storefield Quarries, Northants: Barclay 0–4–0ST No. 20 on a load of ore on December 30, 1966.
[*G. D. King*

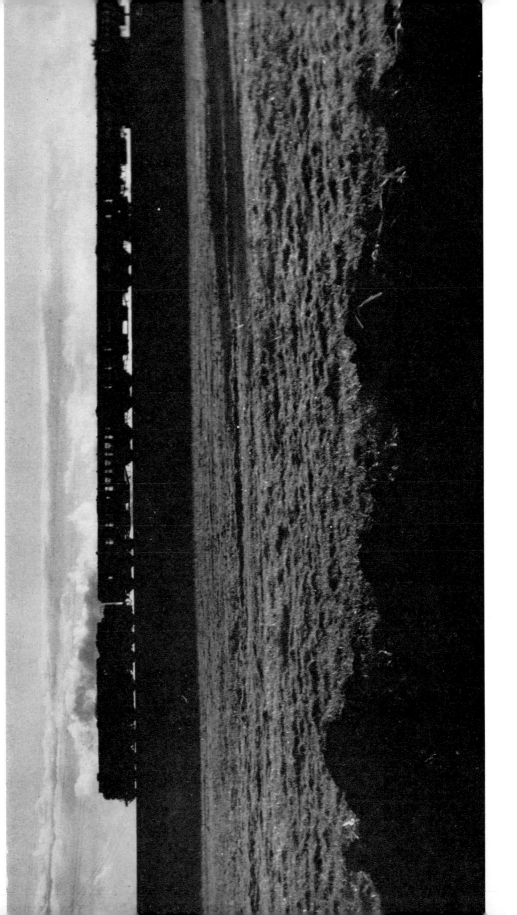

Above: The privately-preserved Class A3 Pacific No. 4472 *Flying Scotsman* emerges from Hadley Wood Tunnel with a down special on May 1, 1967.

[*V. C. K. Allen*

Below: SR "Merchant Navy" Pacific and the 1.25 p.m. Weymouth–Waterloo silhouetted near Christchurch on December 10, 1966.

[*M. Dunnett*

Left : Preserved ex-Caledonian Railway 4–2–2 No. 123 at Glasgow Central on April 19, 1965.   [*P. Hocquard*

Right : Preserved ex-Highland Railway Jones Goods 4–6–0 No. 103 at Dumfries.   [*P. Hocquard*

Below : No. 103 in action—near Kincraig, on the Highland main line, with a Highland Railway Centennial special from Inverness to Perth consisting of two ex-Caledonian Railway coaches, on August 30, 1965.   [*D. Cross*

... the Caledonian Railway 4-2-2 No. 123 makes a dusk departure from Callander with a special in October, 1964.

[W. J. V. Anderson

Below: The Highland Railway Jones Goods 4-6-0 No. 103 tops Beattock summit, Glasgow-bound on its last run before going into inactive preservation, in October, 1965.

[W. J. V. Anderson

Left: Class K1 2–6–0 No. 62052 leaves Fort William with the 5.45 a.m. Glasgow–Mallaig on May 25, 1962. *[M. Mensing*

Below: Class K2 2–6–0 No. 61784 climbs through Glenfinnan with the 10.40 a.m. Fort William–Mallaig goods in April, 1960. *[S. C. Crook*

Above: Keith shed in August, 1960: Class B1 4–6–0 No. 61308 takes the main line with a goods for Aberdeen, while Class J72 0–6–0T No. 68700 shunts the shed yard. Also on view are Class 2 4–4–0 No. 40617, a Class K2 2–6–0 and a Class 5 4–6–0.
[*R. K. Evans*

Right: Caledonian 0–4–4T No. 55263 drifts downhill with the 11.27 a.m. Killin Junction –Killin branch train on August 13, 1960.
[*D. R. Griffin*

Above: A pair of "Crab" 2-6-0s, Nos. 42702 and 42803, double-head a Bargany–Ayr coal train in the Girvan valley in March, 1965.

[*D. Cross*

Facing page, upper: Class Q6 0-8-0 No. 63394 near Blackhall, on the Sunderland–West Hartlepool line, with colliery empties on February 21, 1967.

[*J. R. Hillier*

Facing page, lower: Class B16/3 4-6-0 No. 61437 hauls mineral empties out of Neville Hill, Leeds, on May 28, 1963; Class A1 4-6-2 No. 60124 *Kenilworth* shunts parcels stock in the background.

[*J. M. Rayner*

Above: Class 4 2–6–4T No. 42154 banks "Britannia" Pacific No. 70011 *Hotspur* out of Tebay with a northbound freight on August 25, 1966. [C. Lofth

Left: WR 0–6–2T No. 6697 banks an ore train from Wrexham to Brymbo steelworks on March 12, 1966. [P. Ri

Right: "Big Bertha", the Lickey banker 0–8–0 No. 58100, and "Jinty" 0–6–0T No. 47301 help a Bristol–Birmingham goods train away from Bromsgrove. [F. Spencer Yea

Class ?? 4?-? No. 4?0?0 *Morecambe & Heysham* climbs Beattock bank with a Euston–Glasgow sleeper in July, 1960.

[*W. J. V. Anderson*

Below: Stanier Pacific No. 46254 *City of Stoke-on-Trent* heads an up extra in the moorlands near Low Gill in August, 1964.

[*W. J. V. Anderson*

Above: Class A3 4–6–2 No. 60043 *Brown Jack* heads the 4.20 p.m. to Aberdeen out of Edinburgh Waverley on August 4, 1959.   [K. M. Hill

Left: Class A1 4–6–2 No. 60126 *Sir Vincent Raven* leaves Newcastle Central for the south in May, 1963.   [R. Kell

Below: Class A1 4–6–2s Nos. 60149 *Amadis* and 60130 *Kestrel* at Leeds Central, heading respectively the 5.10 p.m. to Doncaster and 5.30 p.m. to Kings Cross in September, 1961.   [J. M. Rayner

Above: SR "Merchant Navy" 4–6–2 No. 35026 *Lamport & Holt Line* on special
tour duty at Stockport Edgley, November 20, 1966.
[*J. R. Carter*

Right: Winter afternoon and evening at Waterloo: a Class 4 2–6–4T heads for
Nine Elms shed on December 29, 1966 in the upper view; and Class 4 2–6–4T
No. 81040 heads the "Bournemouth Belle" empties, with Class 3 2–6–2T No. 82019
at the next platform, on January 6, 1967.
[*J. H. Bird, D. Mackinnon*

Above: Pickersgill 4–4–0 No. 54486 heads a Blair Atholl–Perth goods south of Murthley in October, 1959.   *[W. J. V. Anderson*

Left, upper: Ex-Highland 0–4–4T No. 55053 approaches Skelbo with the 1 p.m. Dornoch–The Mound branch train in October, 1956.   *[W. J. V. Anderson*

Left, lower: Ex-Caledonian 0–4–4T No. 55195 threads Glenogle with the 4.5 p.m. Callander–Killin school train in September, 1959. The viaduct in the valley to the left carried the Crieff–Balquhidder line.   *[W. J. V. Anderson*

Above: Class A2 Pacific No. 60535 *Hornet's Beauty* crosses the Forth Bridge with the 5.25 p.m. Edinburgh Waverley–Aberdeen on May 9, 1961.

[*C. C. Bowman*

Below: A Class 5 4–6–0 clambers up Beattock bank, assisted by a Class 4 2–6–4T, with a northbound goods in July, 1954.

[*G. F. Heiron*

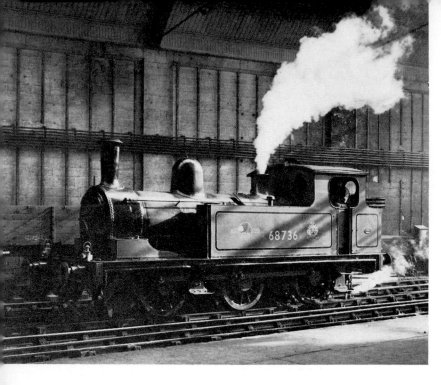

Left, upper: Class J72 0–6–0T No. 68736, painted in NER green livery for station pilot duties, simmers in Newcastle Central in the summer of 1962.

[*A. R. Thompson*

Left, lower: Ex-NBR Class J83 0–6–0T No. 68481 shunts the north end of Edinburgh Waverley station in July, 1958.

[*W. J. V. Anderson*

Right: Ex-NBR Class C15 4–4–2T No. 67452 between Wemyss Castle and Thornton with the 6.7 p.m. from Methil on April 27, 1954.

[*W. J. V. Anderson*

Left, upper Class J27 0–6–0s
rest at North Blyth on August
17, 1966.
[*J. H. Bird*

Left, lower : Two Class Q6
0–8–0s attack the climb to
Annfield with a Consett coal
train on May 19, 1965.
[*M. Dunnett*

Right : Class J27 0–6–0 No.
65894 storms up the 1 in 45
of Seaton bank with coal
empties from Sunderland on
October 29, 1966.
[*P. Riley*

Above: Class B17 4–6–0 No. 61621 *Hatfield House* soon after leaving Ely with the 10.34 a.m. to Peterborough East on May 31, 1958.

[*G. R. Mortimer*

Below: "Patriot" 4–6–0 No. 45533 *Lord Rathmore* heads an evening stopping train to the south near Tebay.

[*W. J. V. Anderson*

Above: SR Class S15 4–6–0 No. 30837 and Class U 2–6–0 No. 31639 assault the 1 in 59 grade south of Alton with an enthusiasts' special on January 16, 1966.

[*P. Riley*

Left: SR Class N 2–6–0 No. 31839 on the 1.18 p.m. Okehampton–Bude crosses the 1.55 p.m. Bude–Halwill Junction, headed by Class 4 2–6–4T No. 80036, at Whitstone & Bridgerule on August 28, 1963.

Above: SR Class W 2–6–4T
No. 31920 gets hold of a
Willesden Junction–Norwood
Junction freight after being
given the road at Clapham
Junction on November
7, 1962.

[*B. Stephenson*

Right: SR Class U 2–6–0
No. 31793 between Withington
and Chedworth with a
Cheltenham–Southampton
train on March 27, 1961.

[*J. S. Gilks*

Left: Class A2 4–6–2 No. 60530 *Sayajirao* climbs past Auchterarder to Gleneagles with the 10 a.m. Dundee–Glasgow on August 30, 1965.

[*P. Riley*

Right, upper: Class A1 4–6–2s Nos. 60121 *Silurian* and 60158 *Aberdonian* come off Gateshead shed over the King Edward Bridge, Newcastle, for duty on October 24, 1964.

[*C. P. Walker*

Below: A Birmingham–Glasgow express, headed by "Princess Royal" 4–6–2 No. 46208 *Princess Helena Victoria,* climbs Beattock from the north.

[*W. J. V. Anderson*

Above: Carnforth shed on June 27, 1966.

[*B. J. Ashworth*

Left: Class V2 2–6–2 No. 60824 is prepared for the road at York shed, May 1, 1966.

[*P. Hocquard*

Below: Bristol Barrow Road shed in October, 1962.

[*G. F. Heiron*

Left: Class K1 2–6–0 No. 62027 comes off the Gateshead line at South Pelaw Junction with a Consett freight on April 3, 1965.

[*M. Dunnett*

Below: WR 4–6–0 No. 6876 *Kingsland Grange* makes a laboured restart with the 6.45 a.m. Salisbury–South Wales freight on January 11, 1964, after stopping for banker at Stapleton Road Junction, Bristol.

[*C. D. Catt*

Right: An SR Class C2X 0–6–0 and Tattenham Corner branch freight near Chipstead Tunnel in October, 1951.

[*B. A. Butt*

Above: Class 9 2–10–0 No. 92213 pounds up Hatton bank with empties for Bordesley yard, Birmingham on October 9, 1965.

[*K. R. Pirt*

Below, left: Class WD 2–8–0 No. 90573 takes the Dore & Totley line at Chinley North Junction with a Gowhole Sidings–Barrow Hill freight on April 22, 1965.

[*J. Clarke*

Below, right: Class 4 2–6–0 No. 43040 shuffles past Carlisle No. 3 box early on an October morning in 1965.

[*P. W. Robinson*

Left: Class J37 0–6–0 No. 64620 approaches Stannergate on December 20, 1966, with the 11.18 a.m. Dundee–Montrose goods—the last regular main-line working by a J37.

[*D. P. Williams*

Below: Class J38 0–6–0 No. 65930 crosses the causeway over Loch Ore on the short branch from Mary Pit to Kelty yard, Fife, in March, 1966.

[*W. J. V. Anderson*

Above: The daily Muirkirk–Carstairs goods ascends the bank out of Inches behind ex-Caledonian Class 3F 0–6–0 No. 57608 on May 10, 1962.

[*D. Cross*

Right: Class J36 0–6–0 No. 65323 negotiates Scotland's Alva branch near Menstrie with a railway enthusiasts' special on April 12, 1963.

[*M. Pope*

Above: "Royal Scot" 4-6-0 No. 46168 *The Girl Guide* tackles the climb to Shap with a Blackpool–Glasgow extra on August 1, 1963.

[*C. P. Walker*

Below: The privately preserved Class A 4-6-2 No. 4498 *Sir Nigel Gresley* threads the Lune Valley with a Crewe–Carlisle special on April 1, 1967.

[*D. E. Gouldthorp*

Above: Class 5 4–6–0 No. 44881 struggles up to Whitrope summit, on the
Waverley route, with the 2.12 p.m. Carlisle Kingmoor–Edinburgh Millerhill
freight on November 4, 1965

[*P. Riley*

Right, upper: The GC line 12.25 p.m. Nottingham–Marylebone semi-fast hurries through
Rothley, between Loughborough and Leicester, on February 24, 1962 behind
Class 5 4–6–0 No. 44821

[*C. P. Walke*

Right, lower: Class 5 4–6–0 with bufferbeam snowplough—No. 45488 near Dunkel
with the 8.20 a.m. Inverness–Perth in April, 1959

[*W. J. V. Anderso*

Left: Class O2 2–8–0 No. 63932 climbs away from the GN main line at High Dyke, Grantham, with iron ore empties for Colsterworth on April 21, 1962.

[*C. P. Walker*

Below: Class O4/1 2–8–0 No. 63585 leaves Colwick yard and passes Gedling Colliery signalbox with a Stanton Ironworks ore train on January 31, 1959.

[*T. Boustead*

Right: WR 2–8–0 No. 3836 wheels an up freight through Birmingham Snow Hill on April 13, 1965.

[*J. H. Cooper-Smith*

Below: Stanier 2–8–0 No. 48456 near Chinley, on the climb to Peak Forest, with a freight from Gow Hole sidings on March 31, 1967.

[*J. H. Cooper-Smith*

Above: Another S & D 2–8–0, No. 53810, climbs out of Bath with the 11 a.m. Evercreech Junction goods on July 12, 1963.

[*C. P. Walker*

Above: Somerset & Dorset 2–8–0 No. 53807 takes water at Evercreech Junction on May 14, 1960.

[*Ivo Peters*

Below: A Templecombe–Bath stopping train, headed by a Class 2 2–6–2T, approaches Combe Down tunnel, south of Bath, in October, 1965.

[*G. F. Heiron*

Following two pages

Left, upper : Class 9 2–10–0 No. 92203 on the up
"Pines Express" crosses Class 4F 0–6–0 No. 44417
and freight at Blandford Forum on August 16, 1960.

[*G. A. Richardson*

Left, lower : Class 4 4–6–0 No. 75072 leaves Bath Green
Park with a stopping train in May, 1965, passing a Class
4 2–6–4T and a class unusual at this station—
"Britannia" Pacific No. 70034 *Thomas Hardy.*

[*Ivo Peters*

Right : Class 4 4–6–0 No. 75072 leaves Evercreech Junction
with the 1.10 p.m. to Bath on January 1, 1966.

[*D. H. Cape*

Left, upper : A Class 3 2–6–2T leaves a trail in the early morning mist as it curves into Mangotsfield with the
7.15 a.m. Bath Green Park–Bristol on September 20, 1965.

[*C. D. Catt*

Left, lower : Another Class 3 2–6–2T No. 82041, enters Warmley station with the 2 p.m. Bath Green Park–Bristol
on November 2, 1963.

[*E. Thomas*

Below : Ex-Midland Class 3F 0–6–0 No. 43216 leaves Cole with an afternoon Highbridge–Templecombe
train on June 30, 1962.

[*D. Cross*

Above: "Clan" Pacific No. 72007 *Clan Mackintosh* near Lamington, in the Clyde Valley, with the 1.30 p.m. Carlisle–Perth in July, 1964.

[*W. J. V. Anderson*

Right: "Britannia" Pacific No. 70027 *Rising Star* darkens the fells as it struggles away from Tebay with an early morning freight on April 1, 1967.

[*J. R. P. Hunt*

Right: Class 9 2-10-0 No. 92177 tops Ais Gill summit, on the Carlisle–Skipton main line, with an up freight on March 25, 1967.

[*W. B. Alexander*

Below: At Blea Moor signalbox Class 5 4-6-0 No. 44902 is on the last mile of the "long drag" to the summit of the Leeds–Carlisle main line with a freight from Brindle Heath on the afternoon of December 20, 1965.

[*J. Clarke*

Facing page: "Jubilee" 4-6-0 No. 45593 *Kolhapur* crosses Dent Head Viaduct after emerging from Blea Moor Tunnel with the 10.15 Leeds–Glasgow on August 20, 1966.

[*M. S. Burns*

POST CARD

The Address only to be written on this side

SCOTTISH GAS BOARD
CENTRALISED ACCOUNTING HEADQUARTERS
GRANTON HOUSE, WEST GRANTON ROAD
EDINBURGH, 5

Dear Customer,

Your usual Meter Reader called today but was unable to obtain a meter reading. He has made an estimate of your gas consumption for which an account based on his estimation will be sent to you, which we trust you will accept on this occasion.

Your Meter Reader will again call in three months time when we hope he will obtain a factual reading which will adjust any variation arising from his estimate of today's reading.

2 / 10 / 68

Customer Accountant.

Left : Class 5 4–6–0 No. 73151, with Caprotti valve gear, restarts a Glasgow–Dundee train from Gleneagles in August, 1964.

[*W. J. V. Anderson*

Below : Class 5 4–6–0 No. 73115 comes up-grade from Addlestone Junction to the SR West of England main line at Byfleet Junction with a Feltham–Eastleigh freight on February 13, 1967.

[*J. H. Bird*

Above: Caprotti Class 5 4-6-0 No. 73147 leaves Perth with the 5.30 p.m. to Glasgow Buchanan Street on May 19, 1965.

[C. W. R. Bowman

Right: Another Caprotti Class 5 4-6-0, No. 73146, on station pilot duty at Glasgow Buchanan Street on April 25, 1965.

[P. H. Groom

Above: "Britannia" Pacific No. 70014 *Iron Duke* storms out of Carlisle on February 5, 1967, with a football supporters' excursion returning from Edinburgh to Wales.   [*A. R. Thompson*

Left, upper: Class A2 4–6–2 No. 60527 *Sun Chariot* heads an Aberdeen express out of Perth in 1963.
                                                                                                    [*W. J. V. Anderson*

Left, lower: An afternoon freight from Edinburgh Millerhill to Perth near Mawcarse, headed by Class A1 4–6–2 No. 60152 *Holyrood*, in March, 1964.   [*W. J. V. Anderson*

Following two pages

Left: A WR "Hall" class 4–6–0 winds up the Golden Valley from Stroud to Sapperton Tunnel with a Cheltenham–Paddington express in July, 1958.
                                                                                                    [*G. F. Heiron*

Right, upper: SR "West Country" 4–6–2 No. 34002 *Salisbury* descends the Slade valley from Mortehoe to Ilfracombe with the 1 a.m. from Waterloo on a May morning in 1964.   [*G. F. Heiron*

Right, lower: SR "Merchant Navy" Pacific No. 35030 *Elder Dempster Lines* hustles the 9.21 a.m. Weymouth–Waterloo through Byfleet & New Haw on February 13, 1967.   [*J. H. Bird*

Above: Class D11 4–4–0 No. 62678 *Luckie Mucklebackit* between Largo and Lundin Links with the 12.46 p.m. Crail–Thornton Junction in August, 1957.
[*W. J. V. Anderson*

Right, upper: Midland compound 4–4–0s at Birmingham New Street in the summer of 1955—No. 40928 at the head of a Leicester train on the left and No. 40932 with a Derby service.
[*A. W. Flowers*

Right, lower: SR "Schools" class 4–4–0 No. 30932 *Blundells* between Chislehurst and St Mary Cray with a Bricklayers Arms–Dover Continental freight on July 31, 1960.
[*D. B. Clark*

Above: Bulleid light Pacific No. 34005 Barnstaple on WR metals near Radley with the northbound "Pines Express" on November 23, 1965.
[W. A. W. Vaughan

Right: SR "Merchant Navy" Pacific No. 35022 Holland-America Line pauses at Salisbury with the up "Atlantic Coast Express" on Easter Monday, 1954.
[G. F. Heiron

Above: SR light Pacific No. 34023 Blackmore Vale restarts an enthusiasts' special from Corfe Castle, on the Swanage branch, on May 7, 1967.

[W. H. Bird

Above: "Crab" 2–6–0 No. 42932 comes off Huddersfield viaduct and approaches the station with a Lancashire-bound freight on July 20, 1962.   [*D. Ian Wood*

Left: Class V3 2–6–2T No. 67675 threads Edinburgh Princes Street gardens with an afternoon suburban train on September 3, 1957.

[*P. H. Groom*

Above: Class 2 2–6–2T No. 84002 shunts the Cheddington–Aylesbury branch, LMR, on May 27, 1961.

Below: Class K3 2–6–0 crosses the LMR–ER boundary at Sherwood Hall, Mansfield, with a Leicester–Scarborough holiday train on August 5, 1961. *[J. Cupit*

Class B1 4-6-0 assaults the climb to Whitrope summit, on the Waverley route, with a Carlisle–Edinburgh special on December 3, 1966.

[M. S. Burns

WR 4-6-0 No. 6996 *Blackwell Hall* passes Stoneycombe on its climb of Dainton bank, west of Newton Abbot, with a down goods on October 29, 1955.

[P. W. Gray

Left, upper : Fowler 2–6–4T No. 42394 approaches Penybont Junction, on the Central Wales line, with the 7.45 a.m. Swansea–Shrewsbury. [*J. S. Gilks*

Left, lower : "Britannia" Pacific No. 70010 *Owen Glendower* heads the 7.15 a.m. Barrow–Preston over Silverdale crossing on June 22, 1966.
[*B. J. Ashworth*

Right, upper : An eastbound Furness freight, with a Class 5 4–6–0 in charge, crosses Kent estuary at Arnside on June 21, 1966. [*B. J. Ashworth*

Right, lower : Class 5 4–6–0 No. 45219 passes Dent, on the Carlisle–Leeds main line, with a south-bound freight on October 14, 1966. [*W. B. Alexander*

Class J27 0-6-0 No. 65885 drifts down from Annfield Plain towards Leadgate, NER, with coal from South Pelaw to Consett in August, 1956

[W. Wake